The Glucose Goddess Smoothie Recipe Book

The Ultimate Guide to Boosting Energy,
Balancing Blood Sugar, and Nourishing Your
Body with Delicious Glucose-Infused Blends

Table of Contents

Introduction

Welcome to the World of Glucose-Rich Smoothies

In a world where health-conscious individuals seek flavorful solutions to nourish their bodies, "The Glucose Goddess Smoothie Recipe Book" emerges as a beacon of wellness. This comprehensive guide is not just another recipe collection; it is a transformative journey into the realms of balanced nutrition, vibrant well-being, and the joy of sipping on delectable smoothies. "The Glucose Goddess Smoothie Recipe Book stands as a testament to our unwavering commitment to fostering well-being through a delightful and nourishing approach. Let's explore the core elements that make it an indispensable resource for anyone dedicated to achieving holistic health."

Glucose Goddess

The term "Glucose Goddess" embodies the spirit of vitality and energy that these smoothies aim to bring into your daily life. Glucose, often referred to as the body's primary source of energy, plays a crucial role in fueling our cells and sustaining an active, vibrant lifestyle. The smoothies featured in this recipe book are thoughtfully curated to incorporate ingredients rich in natural glucose, offering a sustainable and wholesome way to boost your energy levels.

Embracing the Glucose Goddess Lifestyle

At the core of this recipe book lies the fundamental concept of the Glucose Goddess lifestyle—a philosophy dedicated to harmonizing blood sugar levels through the consumption of nutrient-dense and delightful smoothies. Acknowledging the crucial role glucose plays in influencing our energy levels, mood, and overall health, this compilation of recipes is intricately designed to present a seamless fusion of ingredients fostering stable blood sugar levels.

The Science Behind the Smoothies

"The Glucose Goddess Smoothie Recipe Book" is not just a compilation of tasty beverages; it is grounded in scientific principles. Each recipe is carefully designed to incorporate ingredients that help regulate blood sugar, prevent energy crashes, and promote sustained vitality. From fiber-rich fruits to protein-packed nuts, every component is chosen for its nutritional prowess, ensuring that every sip contributes to a healthier, more balanced you.

A Culmination of Culinary Creativity

Beyond the health benefits, this recipe book is a celebration of culinary creativity. The diverse array of smoothie recipes caters to different tastes, preferences, and dietary needs. Whether you are a fan of refreshing green blends, indulgent chocolatey concoctions, or fruity delights, "The Glucose Goddess Smoothie Recipe Book" has something for everyone. Each recipe is a testament to the idea that nourishing your body need not compromise on flavor.

Holistic Wellness for Everyone

The Glucose Goddess lifestyle is not exclusive—it's inclusive. Regardless of age, dietary restrictions, or culinary expertise, this recipe book provides a gateway for everyone to embark on a journey towards holistic wellness. It encourages individuals to embrace the joy of preparing their own nutritious smoothies, fostering a sense of empowerment and ownership over one's health.

Transformative Impact

As we reflect on the past year, stories pour in from individuals who have experienced transformative changes in their lives through the adoption of the Glucose Goddess lifestyle. Weight management, increased energy levels, improved mental clarity—these are just a few of the positive outcomes shared by those who have embraced the smoothie revolution.

Crafting the Perfect Smoothie

Creating a perfect smoothie is an art, and we have endeavored to make it both accessible and enjoyable for everyone. Whether you are a seasoned health enthusiast or just embarking on your wellness journey, "The Glucose Goddess Smoothie Recipe Book" offers a diverse range of recipes that cater to different tastes, preferences, and dietary needs.

From luscious fruit blends to nutrient-packed green concoctions, each recipe is a celebration of flavors, colors, and health benefits. We believe that nourishing your body shouldn't be a chore; it should be a delightful experience that excites your palate and invigorates your senses.

What to Expect in This Journey

In the pages that follow, you will discover a treasure of recipes designed to cater to various dietary requirements, including vegan, gluten-free, and paleo options. We have also incorporated ingredients known for their antioxidant properties, anti-inflammatory benefits, and immune-boosting capabilities, ensuring that your wellness journey is comprehensive and holistic.

"The Glucose Goddess Smoothie Recipe Book" is not just a collection of recipes; it's a guide to making informed and delicious choices that contribute to your overall well-being. Each recipe is accompanied by nutritional information, serving suggestions, and tips for customization, allowing you to tailor your smoothie experience to your unique preferences.

As you embark on this flavorful adventure with us, we invite you to savor the goodness of natural ingredients, embrace the power of glucose-rich foods, and elevate your well-being one delicious sip at a time.

Cheers to a journey of wellness, joy, and the perfect blend of flavors!

With love and health,

Jamie Inchaud

Insights From The Glucose Goddess Book

Maintaining stable blood glucose levels is crucial for overall well-being, and recognizing signs of glucose issues can play a pivotal role in achieving this balance. Simple indicators, such as experiencing energy crashes at 11 a.m. or 3 p.m., struggling with poor sleep quality, facing persistent cravings, finding it challenging to shed excess weight, and noticing visible signs of inflammation like swelling, acne, or redness, may all point to potential glucose imbalances. These signs are not just isolated occurrences; they often contribute to a broader picture of disrupted well-being.

Being overweight can serve as a clear indicator of a glucose imbalance, as excess glucose tends to be stored as fat in the body. Furthermore, disruptions in hunger hormones can lead to rapid shifts from feeling full to hungry, creating a cycle that contributes to weight management difficulties. Common symptoms related to glucose problems, such as energy crashes, a regular need for food, brain fog, and persistent cravings, are often overlooked or attributed to other causes.

The author and brain behind the Glucose Goddess book embarked on a personal journey of self-discovery after overcoming depersonalization-derealization disorder following a severe injury. Her struggles with mental health, accompanied by issues like bad skin and irregular periods, prompted her to delve into the intricate relationship between blood glucose levels and mental well-being. The realization that she was not merely a stranger in her own body but rather deeply connected to its internal workings fueled her curiosity to explore unconventional solutions.

The turning point in her journey came with the discovery of a continuous glucose monitor, a wearable device providing real-time data about blood glucose levels. This technological tool opened her eyes to the direct correlation between stable blood glucose and overall well-being. It became the bridge that connected her physical and mental health, prompting her to experiment with different eating patterns based on research from reputable institutions.

In her pursuit of optimal health, she developed the Glucose Goddess Approach, challenging the conventional notion of good and bad foods. According to her philosophy, no food is inherently good or bad; instead, emphasis is placed on the order in which foods are consumed. The recommended sequence involves starting with veggies and plants, followed by proteins and fats, and concluding with starches and sugars, including desserts. This strategic eating order, backed by scientific studies, has shown to reduce glucose spikes by an impressive 73%.

The Glucose Goddess Book not only encourages a thoughtful approach to eating but also offers unique hacks to enhance one's understanding of their body's response to food. For instance, she suggests consuming vinegar before meals to flatten the glucose curve by 45%. This simple hack underscores the importance of paying attention to the nuances of food intake and its impact on blood glucose levels.

Importantly, the Glucose Goddess Book advocates for a shift in focus from what you eat to how you eat. The author emphasizes that behavioral change doesn't necessarily require immense willpower. Following a consistent meal order—starting with veggies, proceeding to proteins and fats, and concluding with starches and sugars—can serve as a practical and sustainable approach to maintaining stable blood glucose levels.

In conclusion, the key takeaway from the Glucose Goddess Book is a holistic and personalized approach to health. It encourages individuals to listen to their body's signals, understand the impact of food choices on blood glucose levels, and adopt a mindful and intentional way of eating. By prioritizing the order in which foods are consumed and incorporating simple yet effective hacks, individuals can take control of their well-being, paving the way for a healthier and more balanced life. The Glucose Goddess Book serves as a testament to the transformative power of understanding and responding to the body's signals for optimal health and well-being.

Snack Options That Do Not Lead To An Increase In Blood Glucose Levels.

Opt for snacks that won't cause a spike in glucose levels. Optimal choices include savory options, especially when combined with protein and fat if you choose fruit. Consider the following snack ideas:

- Enjoy a handful of baby carrots paired with a spoonful of hummus.
- Indulge in a combination of macadamia nuts and a square of 90% dark chocolate.
- Create a satisfying snack by pairing a hunk of cheese with apple slices smeared with nut butter.
- Opt for bell pepper slices and dip them in a spoonful of guacamole for a flavorful treat.
- Grab a hard-boiled egg and add a dash of hot sauce for a protein-packed snack.
- Delight in lightly salted coconut slivers for a crunchy and satisfying option.
- Choose seeded crackers and pair them with a slice of cheese for a wholesome combination.
- Enjoy a slice of ham for a savory and protein-rich snack.

- Prepare a soft-boiled egg and season it with a dash of salt and pepper for a quick and tasty option.

Smoothie Recipes

Energizing Morning Bliss

Ingredients:

- 1 ripe banana
- 1/2 cup fresh berries (strawberries, blueberries, or raspberries)
- 1/2 cup Greek yogurt
- 1 tablespoon chia seeds
- 1 tablespoon honey
- 1 cup almond milk
- 1/2 cup rolled oats
- Ice cubes (optional)

Instructions:

- Peel and slice the banana.
- In a blender, combine banana slices, fresh berries, Greek yogurt, chia seeds, honey, almond milk, and rolled oats.
- Blend on high until smooth and creamy.
- Add ice cubes if desired and blend again for a refreshing chill.
- Pour into a glass and enjoy your Energizing Morning Bliss smoothie!

Berry-Pomegranate Powerhouse

Ingredients:

- 1 cup mixed berries (strawberries, blueberries, raspberries)
- 1/2 cup pomegranate seeds
- 1 ripe banana
- 1/2 cup Greek yogurt
- 1 tablespoon chia seeds
- 1 cup spinach leaves
- 1 cup almond milk
- Ice cubes (optional)

Instructions:

- Add mixed berries, pomegranate seeds, ripe banana, Greek yogurt, chia seeds, and spinach leaves to a blender.
- Pour in almond milk.
- Blend on high speed until smooth and creamy.
- If desired, add ice cubes and blend again for a refreshing chill.
- Pour into a glass and enjoy the Berry-Pomegranate Powerhouse for a nutritious boost to your day!

Cocoa-Almond Delight

Ingredients for Cocoa-Almond Delight:
- 1 banana (ripe)
- 1 cup almond milk
- 2 tablespoons almond butter
- 1 tablespoon cocoa powder
- 1 tablespoon honey or maple syrup (optional, for sweetness)
- Ice cubes (optional)

Instructions:

- Peel the ripe banana and place it in a blender.
- Add almond milk, almond butter, cocoa powder, and sweetener (if using).
- Blend the ingredients until smooth and creamy.
- If desired, add ice cubes and blend again for a refreshing chill.
- Pour the Cocoa-Almond Delight into a glass and enjoy the rich, chocolaty goodness of this energizing smoothie!

Mango-Turmeric Tropical Boost

Ingredients
- 1 cup frozen mango chunks
- 1 banana

- 1/2 cup pineapple chunks
- 1/2 teaspoon turmeric powder
- 1 tablespoon chia seeds
- 1 cup coconut water

Instructions:
- Place frozen mango chunks, banana, pineapple chunks, turmeric powder, and chia seeds in a blender.
- Add coconut water to the blender.
- Blend all the ingredients until smooth and creamy.
- Pour the smoothie into a glass and enjoy your Mango-Turmeric Tropical Boost, packed with vibrant flavors and health-boosting properties.

Blueberry-Lemon Zest Refresher

Ingredients:

- 1 cup fresh or frozen blueberries
- 1 ripe banana
- 1/2 cup Greek yogurt
- 1 tablespoon honey
- 1 teaspoon grated lemon zest
- 1 cup almond milk
- Ice cubes (optional)

Instructions:

- In a blender, combine blueberries, banana, Greek yogurt, honey, and grated lemon zest.
- Pour in almond milk to the mixture.
- Blend on high speed until smooth and creamy.
- Add ice cubes if desired and blend again for a refreshing chill.
- Pour into a glass and garnish with a few blueberries or a twist of lemon zest.
- Enjoy your Blueberry-Lemon Zest Refresher as a delicious and energizing smoothie!

Avocado-Kale Green Goddess

Ingredients:
- 1 ripe avocado
- 1 cup kale leaves, stems removed
- 1/2 banana
- 1/2 cup pineapple chunks
- 1 tablespoon chia seeds
- 1 cup unsweetened almond milk
- Ice cubes (optional)

Instructions:
- Peel and pit the avocado. Rinse the kale leaves and remove the stems. Peel the banana and cut it into halves. Gather pineapple chunks and chia seeds.

- In a blender, combine avocado, kale, banana, pineapple chunks, chia seeds, and almond milk.
- Blend the ingredients until smooth and creamy. Add ice cubes if you prefer a colder smoothie.
- Pour the green goodness into a glass and enjoy your Avocado-Kale Green Goddess smoothie packed with nutrients to kickstart your day!

Strawberry-Basil Bliss

Ingredients:
- 1 cup fresh strawberries, hulled
- 1 banana, peeled
- 1/2 cup Greek yogurt
- 1 tablespoon honey
- 1/2 teaspoon vanilla extract
- 5-6 fresh basil leaves
- 1/2 cup ice cubes
- 1/2 cup water or almond milk (adjust for desired consistency)

Instructions:
- In a blender, combine fresh strawberries, banana, Greek yogurt, honey, vanilla extract, basil leaves, and ice cubes.
- Add water or almond milk to achieve your preferred smoothie consistency.
- Blend until smooth and creamy.

- Pour into a glass and garnish with a strawberry slice or basil leaf if desired.
- Enjoy your Strawberry-Basil Bliss – a refreshing and nutritious smoothie to kickstart your day!

Cherry-Vanilla Dream

Ingredients:
- 1 cup frozen cherries
- 1 ripe banana
- 1/2 cup Greek yogurt
- 1 cup almond milk
- 1 teaspoon vanilla extract
- 1 tablespoon honey or maple syrup (optional)
- Ice cubes (optional)

Instructions:
- Combine frozen cherries, ripe banana, Greek yogurt, almond milk, and vanilla extract in a blender.
- Blend until smooth and creamy.
- Taste and add honey or maple syrup if additional sweetness is desired.
- If you prefer a colder consistency, add ice cubes and blend again.
- Pour into a glass and enjoy your Cherry-Vanilla Dream smoothie as a refreshing and delightful treat.

Peach-Ginger Elixir

Ingredients:
- 2 ripe peaches, peeled and sliced
- 1-inch piece of fresh ginger, peeled and grated
- 1 cup plain Greek yogurt
- 1 tablespoon honey
- 1/2 cup almond milk
- 1 tablespoon chia seeds (optional)
- Ice cubes

Instructions:
- In a blender, combine sliced peaches, grated ginger, Greek yogurt, honey, and almond milk.
- Blend on high until smooth and creamy.
- If desired, add chia seeds for an extra nutritional boost and blend briefly.
- Add ice cubes and blend again until the mixture is chilled and refreshing.
- Pour into glasses and garnish with a slice of peach or a sprinkle of chia seeds, if desired.
- Enjoy your Peach-Ginger Elixir as a nutritious and revitalizing drink!

Raspberry-Coconut Zen Blend

Ingredients:

- 1 cup fresh or frozen raspberries
- 1/2 cup coconut milk
- 1/2 cup Greek yogurt
- 1 tablespoon honey
- 1 tablespoon chia seeds
- 1/2 teaspoon vanilla extract
- Ice cubes (optional)

Instructions:
- In a blender, combine raspberries, coconut milk, Greek yogurt, honey, chia seeds, and vanilla extract.
- Blend until smooth and creamy.
- If desired, add ice cubes and blend again for a refreshing chill.
- Pour the Raspberry-Coconut Zen Blend into a glass.
- Garnish with additional raspberries or a sprinkle of chia seeds if you like.
- Sip and enjoy this delightful, nutritious smoothie!

Banana-Peanut Butter Power Punch

Ingredients:
- 2 ripe bananas
- 2 tablespoons peanut butter
- 1 cup Greek yogurt
- 1 cup almond milk

- 1 tablespoon honey
- 1/2 teaspoon cinnamon
- Ice cubes (optional)

Instructions:
- Peel and slice the ripe bananas.
- In a blender, combine bananas, peanut butter, Greek yogurt, almond milk, honey, and cinnamon.
- Blend until smooth and creamy.
- Add ice cubes if desired and blend again until the desired consistency is reached.
- Pour into a glass and enjoy the power-packed goodness of this banana-peanut butter smoothie!

Cranberry-Orange Citrus Splash

Ingredients:
- 1 cup fresh cranberries
- 1 orange, peeled and segmented
- 1 banana
- 1/2 cup Greek yogurt
- 1 tablespoon honey
- 1 cup orange juice
- Ice cubes (optional)

Instructions:

- Combine fresh cranberries, orange segments, banana, Greek yogurt, and honey in a blender.
- Pour in orange juice to enhance the citrus flavor.
- Blend until smooth and creamy.
- Add ice cubes if desired and blend again for a refreshing chill.
- Pour into a glass and garnish with a slice of orange or a few cranberries.
- Sip and enjoy your Cranberry-Orange Citrus Splash – a vibrant and nutritious start to your day!

Minty Melon Cooler

Ingredients:
- 2 cups diced watermelon
- 1 cup diced honeydew melon
- 1/2 cup fresh mint leaves
- 1 cup coconut water
- 1 tablespoon honey
- Ice cubes (optional)

Instructions:
- Combine watermelon, honeydew melon, and fresh mint leaves in a blender.
- Add coconut water and honey to the blender.
- Blend until smooth and well combined.

- Optionally, add ice cubes for a cooler consistency.
- Pour into glasses and garnish with mint leaves.
- Enjoy your refreshing Minty Melon Cooler!

Kiwi-Berry Burst

Ingredients:
- 2 ripe kiwis, peeled and sliced
- 1 cup mixed berries (strawberries, blueberries, raspberries)
- 1 ripe banana
- 1/2 cup Greek yogurt
- 1 tablespoon honey
- 1 cup unsweetened almond milk
- Ice cubes (optional)

Instructions:
- Place kiwis, mixed berries, banana, Greek yogurt, and honey in a blender.
- Add almond milk to the mixture.
- Blend until smooth and creamy.
- If desired, add ice cubes and blend again for a refreshing chill.
- Pour into glasses and garnish with kiwi slices or berries.

- Enjoy your vibrant and nutritious Kiwi-Berry Burst Smoothie!

Apple-Cinnamon Crunch

Ingredients
- 1 medium-sized apple, peeled, cored, and diced
- 1/2 cup rolled oats
- 1/2 cup Greek yogurt
- 1 cup almond milk
- 1 tablespoon honey or maple syrup
- 1/2 teaspoon ground cinnamon
- Ice cubes (optional)

Instructions:
- In a blender, combine the diced apple, rolled oats, Greek yogurt, almond milk, honey or maple syrup, and ground cinnamon.
- Blend the ingredients on high speed until smooth and creamy.
- If desired, add ice cubes and blend again until the smoothie reaches your preferred consistency.
- Pour the Apple-Cinnamon Crunch smoothie into a glass.
- Optionally, garnish with a sprinkle of cinnamon or a few apple slices for an extra touch.
- Enjoy your energizing and delicious Apple-Cinnamon Crunch smoothie!

Grapefruit-Goji Berry Revitalizer

Ingredients:
- 1 cup fresh grapefruit juice
- 1/2 cup frozen mixed berries (including goji berries)
- 1 banana, peeled and sliced
- 1/2 cup Greek yogurt
- 1 tablespoon honey
- 1/2 cup ice cubes

Instructions:
- In a blender, combine fresh grapefruit juice and frozen mixed berries.
- Add sliced banana, Greek yogurt, and honey to the blender.
- Toss in ice cubes for a refreshing chill.
- Blend on high speed until smooth and creamy.
- Pour the revitalizing smoothie into a glass and enjoy your Grapefruit-Goji Berry Revitalizer!

Tip: Adjust the thickness by adding more juice or ice cubes as desired. Cheers to a vibrant and energizing start!

Fig-Walnut Wonder Smoothie

Ingredients:

- 1 cup fresh figs, stemmed and halved
- 1/2 cup walnuts
- 1 banana, peeled and sliced
- 1 cup Greek yogurt
- 1 tablespoon honey
- 1/2 teaspoon cinnamon
- 1 cup almond milk
- Ice cubes (optional)

Instructions:
- In a blender, combine fresh figs, walnuts, banana, Greek yogurt, honey, and cinnamon.
- Pour in almond milk to achieve the desired consistency.
- Blend until smooth and creamy.
- If you prefer a colder smoothie, add ice cubes and blend again.
- Pour into a glass and garnish with a slice of fig or a sprinkle of chopped walnuts if desired.
- Enjoy your Fig-Walnut Wonder, a delightful and nutritious smoothie to kickstart your day!

Cantaloupe-Carrot Sunrise

Ingredients:
- 1 cup diced cantaloupe

- 1 medium carrot, peeled and sliced
- 1/2 cup orange juice
- 1/2 cup Greek yogurt
- 1 tablespoon honey
- Ice cubes (optional)

Instructions:
- In a blender, combine diced cantaloupe, sliced carrot, and Greek yogurt.
- Add orange juice and honey to the mixture.
- Blend until smooth and creamy.
- If desired, add ice cubes and blend again for a refreshing chill.
- Pour into a glass and enjoy your Cantaloupe-Carrot Sunrise for a nutritious start to your day!

Papaya-Coconut Bliss

Ingredients:

- 1 cup ripe papaya, peeled, seeded, and diced
- 1/2 cup coconut milk
- 1/2 cup Greek yogurt
- 1 tablespoon honey
- 1/2 teaspoon vanilla extract
- Ice cubes (optional)
- Shredded coconut for garnish (optional)

Instructions:

- In a blender, combine diced papaya, coconut milk, Greek yogurt, honey, and vanilla extract.
- Blend until smooth and creamy.
- If desired, add ice cubes and blend again for a refreshing chill.
- Pour into a glass and garnish with shredded coconut if you like.
- Serve immediately and enjoy your tropical Papaya-Coconut Bliss smoothie!

Apricot-Almond Euphoria

Ingredients for Apricot-Almond Euphoria Smoothie:

- 1 cup frozen apricots
- 1 banana, peeled
- 1/4 cup almonds, preferably unsalted
- 1 cup Greek yogurt
- 1 tablespoon honey
- 1/2 cup almond milk
- Ice cubes (optional)

Instructions:

- In a blender, combine frozen apricots, banana, almonds, Greek yogurt, and honey.
- Pour in almond milk to enhance the smoothness.

- If you prefer a colder texture, add a handful of ice cubes.
- Blend until the mixture reaches a smooth and creamy consistency.
- Taste and adjust sweetness by adding more honey if desired.
- Pour into a glass, garnish with sliced almonds or apricots if you like.
- Enjoy your Apricot-Almond Euphoria smoothie as a delicious and nutrient-packed treat!

Blackberry-Sage Serenity

Ingredients
- 1 cup blackberries (fresh or frozen)
- 1 medium banana, peeled and sliced
- 1/2 cup Greek yogurt (or non-dairy alternative)
- 1 tablespoon chia seeds
- 1 teaspoon fresh sage leaves
- 1 cup almond milk (or any preferred milk)
- Ice cubes (optional)

Instructions:
- Wash the blackberries and sage leaves. Peel and slice the banana.

- In a blender, combine blackberries, banana slices, Greek yogurt, chia seeds, fresh sage leaves, and almond milk.
- Blend on high speed until the mixture is smooth and creamy. Add ice cubes if you prefer a colder consistency.
- If the smoothie is too thick, add more almond milk in small increments until desired consistency is reached.
- Pour the smoothie into a glass and garnish with a few fresh sage leaves or blackberries if desired.
- Sip and savor the delightful combination of blackberries and sage for a refreshing and serene start to your day!

Pear-Cardamom Delicacy

Ingredients:
- 2 ripe pears, peeled and diced
- 1 banana, peeled
- 1 cup Greek yogurt
- 1 tablespoon honey
- 1/2 teaspoon ground cardamom
- 1 cup almond milk
- Ice cubes (optional)

Instructions:

- In a blender, combine the diced pears, banana, Greek yogurt, honey, and ground cardamom.
- Add almond milk to the mixture to achieve the desired consistency.
- If you prefer a colder smoothie, you can add ice cubes to the blender.
- Blend all the ingredients until smooth and creamy.
- Pour the Pear-Cardamom Delicacy into glasses and enjoy this refreshing and flavorful smoothie!

Cinnamon-Raisin Radiance

Ingredients:

- 1 cup almond milk
- 1 banana, frozen
- 1/2 cup raisins
- 1/2 teaspoon ground cinnamon
- 1 tablespoon chia seeds
- 1 tablespoon honey or maple syrup
- Ice cubes (optional)

Instructions:

- In a blender, combine almond milk, frozen banana, raisins, ground cinnamon, chia seeds, and honey/maple syrup.
- Blend until smooth and creamy.

- Add ice cubes if a colder consistency is desired, then blend again.
- Pour into a glass and garnish with a sprinkle of cinnamon or a few raisins if desired.
- Enjoy your Cinnamon-Raisin Radiance smoothie for a delicious and energizing start to your day!

Mango-Basil Breeze

Ingredients
- 1 cup frozen mango chunks
- 1/2 cup fresh basil leaves
- 1/2 banana
- 1/2 cup Greek yogurt
- 1 tablespoon honey
- 1 cup coconut water
- Ice cubes (optional)

Instructions:
- Combine frozen mango chunks, fresh basil leaves, banana, Greek yogurt, and honey in a blender.
- Add coconut water to the mixture.
- Blend all ingredients until smooth and creamy.
- If desired, add ice cubes for a cooler texture.
- Pour the smoothie into a glass and garnish with a basil leaf.

- Enjoy your refreshing Mango-Basil Breeze!

Plum-Hemp Harmony

Ingredients for Plum-Hemp Harmony:
- 1 cup fresh plums, pitted and sliced
- 1 ripe banana
- 1/2 cup Greek yogurt
- 1 tablespoon hemp seeds
- 1 tablespoon honey
- 1/2 cup almond milk
- Ice cubes (optional)

Instructions:
- In a blender, combine fresh plums, banana, Greek yogurt, hemp seeds, honey, and almond milk.
- Blend until smooth and creamy.
- If desired, add ice cubes and blend again for a refreshing chill.
- Pour the smoothie into a glass and garnish with additional hemp seeds or a plum slice if you like.
- Enjoy your Plum-Hemp Harmony as a nutritious and delicious smoothie!

Chia-Cherry Chiller

Ingredients:

- 1 cup frozen cherries
- 1 tablespoon chia seeds
- 1/2 cup Greek yogurt
- 1 cup almond milk
- 1 tablespoon honey or maple syrup (optional)
- Ice cubes (optional)

Instructions:
- In a blender, combine frozen cherries, chia seeds, Greek yogurt, and almond milk.
- If desired, add honey or maple syrup for sweetness.
- Blend until smooth and creamy.
- For a colder consistency, add ice cubes and blend again.
- Pour into a glass, garnish with a few whole cherries or a sprinkle of chia seeds.
- Enjoy your refreshing and nutrient-packed Chia-Cherry Chiller!

Turkish Delight Smoothie

Ingredients:
- 1 cup frozen mixed berries (strawberries, raspberries, blueberries)
- 1 ripe banana
- 1/2 cup plain Greek yogurt
- 1 tablespoon honey

- 1/2 teaspoon rose water
- 1 cup almond milk
- Ice cubes (optional)

Instructions:

- In a blender, combine frozen berries, ripe banana, Greek yogurt, honey, and rose water.
- Pour in almond milk to the mixture.
- Blend on high speed until smooth and creamy.
- Add ice cubes if a colder consistency is desired, and blend again.
- Pour into a glass and garnish with a sprinkle of crushed pistachios or edible rose petals for a delightful Turkish touch.
- Enjoy your refreshing Turkish Delight Smoothie!

Blue Spirulina Elixir

Ingredients:

- 1 cup almond milk
- 1 ripe banana
- 1/2 cup blueberries (fresh or frozen)
- 1 tablespoon chia seeds
- 1 teaspoon blue spirulina powder
- 1 tablespoon honey or maple syrup (optional)
- Ice cubes (optional)

Instructions:

- In a blender, combine almond milk, banana, blueberries, chia seeds, and blue spirulina powder.
- Blend until smooth and creamy.
- Taste and add honey or maple syrup if additional sweetness is desired.
- If you prefer a colder consistency, add ice cubes and blend again.
- Pour into a glass, garnish with additional blueberries or a slice of banana if desired.
- Enjoy your refreshing and nutrient-packed Blue Spirulina Elixir!

Pomegranate-Beet Bliss

Ingredients
- 1 cup pomegranate seeds
- 1 small beet, peeled and chopped
- 1 banana
- 1/2 cup Greek yogurt
- 1 tablespoon chia seeds
- 1 teaspoon honey (optional)
- 1 cup cold water or coconut water
- Ice cubes (optional)

Instructions:

- Combine pomegranate seeds, chopped beet, banana, Greek yogurt, and chia seeds in a blender.
- Add honey if desired for sweetness.
- Pour in cold water or coconut water to aid in blending.
- Blend until smooth and creamy.
- If a colder consistency is preferred, add ice cubes and blend again.
- Pour the smoothie into a glass and enjoy the vibrant and nutritious Pomegranate-Beet Bliss!

Vanilla-Fig Infusion

Ingredients
- 1 cup fresh figs, sliced
- 1 frozen banana
- 1 cup unsweetened almond milk
- 1 teaspoon vanilla extract
- 1 tablespoon chia seeds
- 1 tablespoon honey or maple syrup (optional, for added sweetness)
- Ice cubes (optional)

Instructions:
- Place the sliced fresh figs, frozen banana, almond milk, vanilla extract, chia seeds, and optional sweetener in a blender.

- Blend the ingredients on high speed until the mixture is smooth and creamy.
- If a thicker consistency is desired, add ice cubes and blend again until well combined.
- Pour the Vanilla-Fig Infusion into a glass and garnish with additional fig slices or a drizzle of honey if desired.
- Enjoy your delicious and nutritious Vanilla-Fig Infusion as a refreshing beverage or a healthy snack!

Passionfruit-Coconut Dream

Ingredients for Passionfruit-Coconut Dream Smoothie:
- 1 cup fresh passionfruit pulp
- 1/2 cup coconut milk
- 1 banana, frozen
- 1/2 cup Greek yogurt
- 1 tablespoon honey
- 1/2 cup ice cubes

Instructions:
- Scoop out 1 cup of fresh passionfruit pulp and place it in a blender.
- Add 1/2 cup of coconut milk to the blender.
- Toss in a frozen banana for a creamy texture.

- Spoon in 1/2 cup of Greek yogurt for added richness.
- Drizzle 1 tablespoon of honey into the mix for sweetness.
- Finally, add 1/2 cup of ice cubes to chill and blend everything until smooth.
- Pour into a glass and enjoy your refreshing Passionfruit-Coconut Dream smoothie!

Hazelnut-Chocolate Bliss

Ingredients:
- 1 ripe banana
- 1 cup hazelnut milk
- 2 tablespoons cocoa powder
- 1 tablespoon almond butter
- 1 teaspoon honey or maple syrup (optional)
- 1/2 teaspoon vanilla extract
- Ice cubes (optional)

Instructions:
- Peel and slice the ripe banana.
- In a blender, combine banana slices, hazelnut milk, cocoa powder, almond butter, and vanilla extract.
- Add honey or maple syrup for sweetness if desired.

- Blend on high speed until the mixture is smooth and creamy.
- If you prefer a colder smoothie, add a handful of ice cubes and blend again.
- Pour the Hazelnut-Chocolate Bliss into a glass and enjoy this indulgent and energizing treat!

Raspberry-Mint Medley

Ingredients:
- 1 cup fresh raspberries
- 1 banana, peeled and sliced
- 1/2 cup Greek yogurt
- 1/4 cup fresh mint leaves
- 1 tablespoon honey
- 1 cup almond milk
- Ice cubes (optional)

Instructions:
- In a blender, combine raspberries, banana, Greek yogurt, mint leaves, honey, and almond milk.
- Blend until smooth and creamy.
- If desired, add ice cubes and blend again for a refreshing chill.
- Pour into a glass and garnish with a mint sprig.
- Enjoy your revitalizing Raspberry-Mint Medley smoothie!

Dragon Fruit-Pineapple Fusion

Ingredients:
- 1 cup dragon fruit, diced
- 1 cup pineapple chunks
- 1 banana, peeled
- 1/2 cup Greek yogurt
- 1 tablespoon chia seeds
- 1 cup coconut water
- Ice cubes (optional)

Instructions:
- In a blender, combine diced dragon fruit, pineapple chunks, peeled banana, Greek yogurt, and chia seeds.
- Add coconut water to the mixture.
- Blend until smooth and creamy.
- If desired, add ice cubes and blend again for a refreshing chill.
- Pour into a glass and enjoy this tropical Dragon Fruit-Pineapple Fusion Smoothie!

Cucumber-Melon Cooler

Ingredients:
- 1 cup cucumber, peeled and diced
- 1 cup honeydew melon, cubed
- 1/2 cup plain Greek yogurt
- 1 tablespoon honey

- 1 cup ice cubes
- 1/2 cup cold water
- Fresh mint leaves for garnish (optional)

Instructions:
- In a blender, combine cucumber, honeydew melon, Greek yogurt, honey, and ice cubes.
- Blend on high speed until smooth and creamy.
- Add cold water gradually while blending until you achieve the desired consistency.
- Pour the smoothie into glasses and garnish with fresh mint leaves if desired.
- Serve immediately and enjoy the refreshing Cucumber-Melon Cooler!

Cranberry-Walnut Wellness

Ingredients:
- 1 cup cranberries (fresh or frozen)
- 1/2 cup walnuts
- 1 banana, ripe
- 1 cup Greek yogurt
- 1 tablespoon honey
- 1/2 cup almond milk
- Ice cubes (optional)

Instructions:
- In a blender, combine cranberries, walnuts, banana, Greek yogurt, and honey.

- Add almond milk to the mix for a creamy consistency.
- Blend the ingredients until smooth.
- If desired, add ice cubes and blend again for a refreshing chill.
- Pour into a glass and enjoy your Cranberry-Walnut Wellness smoothie for a nutrient-packed and delicious start to your day!

Mango-Turmeric Sunrise

- Ingredients:
- 1 ripe mango, peeled and diced
- 1 banana, peeled and sliced
- 1 cup orange juice
- 1/2 cup Greek yogurt
- 1 teaspoon turmeric powder
- 1 tablespoon honey
- Ice cubes (optional)

Instructions:
- In a blender, combine the diced mango, sliced banana, orange juice, Greek yogurt, turmeric powder, and honey.
- Blend until smooth and creamy.
- If desired, add ice cubes and blend again for a refreshing chill.

- Pour the smoothie into glasses and enjoy your Mango-Turmeric Sunrise, a vibrant and nutrient-rich way to start your day!

Cherry-Almond Euphoria

Ingredients:
- 1 cup frozen cherries
- 1 ripe banana
- 1/2 cup almond milk
- 1/4 cup Greek yogurt
- 1 tablespoon almond butter
- 1 teaspoon honey (optional)
- Ice cubes (optional)

Instructions:
- In a blender, combine frozen cherries, ripe banana, almond milk, Greek yogurt, and almond butter.
- If desired, add a teaspoon of honey for sweetness.
- Blend on high until smooth and creamy.
- If a colder consistency is preferred, add ice cubes and blend again.
- Pour into a glass and enjoy the Cherry-Almond Euphoria - a deliciously energizing smoothie!

Strawberry-Basil Serenity

Ingredients:
- 1 cup fresh strawberries, hulled
- 1 banana, peeled
- 1/2 cup Greek yogurt
- 1/4 cup fresh basil leaves
- 1 tablespoon honey
- 1 cup ice cubes
- 1/2 cup almond milk (or any milk of your choice)

Instructions:
- In a blender, combine strawberries, banana, Greek yogurt, basil leaves, and honey.
- Add ice cubes and pour in almond milk.
- Blend on high speed until smooth and creamy.
- Taste and adjust sweetness if needed by adding more honey.
- Pour into a glass and garnish with a basil leaf for a refreshing touch.
- Enjoy your Strawberry-Basil Serenity smoothie as a delightful and nutritious treat!

Pear-Ginger Zest

Ingredients for Pear-Ginger Zest Smoothie:
- 2 ripe pears, peeled and chopped

- 1-inch piece of fresh ginger, peeled and grated
- 1 cup spinach leaves
- 1 banana, peeled
- 1 cup almond milk (or any preferred milk)
- 1 tablespoon chia seeds
- Ice cubes (optional)

Instructions:

- Place chopped pears, grated ginger, spinach, banana, and almond milk in a blender.
- Blend until smooth and creamy.
- Add chia seeds and blend briefly to incorporate.
- If desired, add ice cubes for a refreshing chill.
- Pour into a glass and garnish with a slice of pear or a sprinkle of chia seeds.
- Sip and enjoy the invigorating blend of pear and ginger zest to kickstart your day!

Blueberry-Lavender Lavish

Ingredients

- 1 cup blueberries (fresh or frozen)
- 1 banana, peeled and sliced
- 1/2 cup plain Greek yogurt
- 1 tablespoon honey
- 1 teaspoon dried lavender flowers
- 1 cup almond milk (or any milk of your choice)
- Ice cubes (optional)

Instructions:

- In a blender, combine the blueberries, sliced banana, Greek yogurt, honey, and dried lavender flowers.
- Pour in the almond milk.
- If desired, add a handful of ice cubes for a refreshing chill.
- Blend on high speed until the mixture is smooth and creamy.
- Pour the Blueberry-Lavender Lavish into a glass.
- Garnish with a few extra blueberries or a sprinkle of lavender flowers if you like.
- Enjoy your delicious and nutrient-packed Blueberry-Lavender Lavish!

Peach-Cinnamon Celebration

Ingredients:

- - 2 ripe peaches, peeled and sliced
- - 1 banana
- - 1 cup Greek yogurt
- - 1/2 teaspoon cinnamon
- - 1 tablespoon honey
- - 1 cup almond milk
- - Ice cubes (optional)

Instructions:

- 1. Place peaches, banana, Greek yogurt, cinnamon, honey, and almond milk in a blender.
- 2. Blend until smooth and creamy.
- 3. Add ice cubes if desired and blend again.
- 4. Pour into a glass and garnish with a sprinkle of cinnamon.
- 5. Enjoy your Peach-Cinnamon Celebration smoothie!

Orange-Turmeric Radiance

Ingredients:
- 2 oranges, peeled and segmented
- 1 banana, peeled
- 1/2 teaspoon turmeric powder
- 1 tablespoon honey
- 1 cup Greek yogurt
- 1/2 cup almond milk
- Ice cubes (optional)

Instructions:
- Place oranges, banana, turmeric powder, honey, Greek yogurt, and almond milk in a blender.
- Blend until smooth and creamy.
- Add ice cubes if desired and blend again for a refreshing chill.

- Pour into a glass and savor the vibrant, nutrient-packed Orange-Turmeric Radiance smoothie.

Apple-Cranberry Crunch

Ingredients:
- 1 cup fresh cranberries
- 1 medium-sized apple, peeled and diced
- 1/2 cup rolled oats
- 1 tablespoon honey
- 1 cup Greek yogurt
- 1/2 cup almond milk
- Ice cubes (optional)

Instructions:
- Combine cranberries, diced apple, rolled oats, honey, Greek yogurt, and almond milk in a blender.
- Blend until smooth and creamy.
- If desired, add ice cubes and blend again for a refreshing chill.
- Pour into a glass, and enjoy your Apple-Cranberry Crunch smoothie!

Vanilla-Bean Extravaganza

Ingredients:
- 1 cup almond milk
- 1 frozen banana
- 1 tablespoon almond butter
- 1 teaspoon chia seeds
- 1/2 vanilla bean (seeds scraped)
- 1/2 teaspoon honey or maple syrup (optional)
- Ice cubes (optional)

Instructions:
- In a blender, combine almond milk, frozen banana, almond butter, chia seeds, and vanilla bean seeds.
- Blend until smooth and creamy.
- Taste and add honey or maple syrup if desired for sweetness.
- Optional: Add ice cubes and blend again for a colder texture.
- Pour into a glass and enjoy your Vanilla-Bean Extravaganza!

Mint Chocolate Avocado Indulgence

Ingredients:
- 1 ripe avocado
- 1 cup spinach leaves
- 1 banana, frozen

- 1 tablespoon cocoa powder
- 1 tablespoon honey or maple syrup
- 1/2 teaspoon peppermint extract
- 1 cup almond milk
- Ice cubes (optional)

Instructions:
- Combine avocado, spinach, frozen banana, cocoa powder, honey or maple syrup, and peppermint extract in a blender.
- Add almond milk to the mix.
- Blend until smooth and creamy.
- If desired, add ice cubes and blend again.
- Pour into a glass, and enjoy your Mint Chocolate Avocado Indulgence!

Kiwi-Coconut Green Oasis

Ingredients
- 2 ripe kiwis
- 1/2 cup coconut water
- 1 cup fresh spinach leaves
- 1/2 banana
- 1/2 cup Greek yogurt
- Ice cubes (optional)

Instructions:
- Peel and slice the kiwis.

- In a blender, combine kiwis, coconut water, spinach, banana, and Greek yogurt.
- Blend until smooth and creamy.
- Add ice cubes if desired and blend again.
- Pour into a glass and enjoy your refreshing Kiwi-Coconut Green Oasis!

Almond Joy Delight

Ingredients:
- 1 cup almond milk
- 1 ripe banana
- 2 tablespoons cocoa powder
- 1/4 cup shredded coconut
- 1 tablespoon almond butter
- 1 teaspoon honey or maple syrup (optional)
- Ice cubes (optional)

Instructions:
- In a blender, combine almond milk, banana, cocoa powder, shredded coconut, and almond butter.
- If desired, add honey or maple syrup for sweetness.
- Blend until smooth and creamy.
- For a colder treat, add ice cubes and blend again.
- Pour into a glass, garnish with extra shredded coconut, and enjoy your Almond Joy Delight!

Ginger-Pineapple Turmeric Tonic

Ingredients:
- 1 cup pineapple chunks
- 1 teaspoon grated ginger
- 1/2 teaspoon turmeric powder
- 1 banana
- 1 cup coconut water
- Ice cubes (optional)

Instructions:
- Combine pineapple chunks, grated ginger, turmeric powder, banana, and coconut water in a blender.
- Blend until smooth.
- Add ice cubes if desired and blend again.
- Pour into a glass and enjoy the refreshing Ginger-Pineapple Turmeric Tonic!

Blackberry-Peach Pleasure

Ingredients
- 1 cup blackberries
- 1 ripe peach, peeled and sliced
- 1/2 cup Greek yogurt
- 1 tablespoon honey
- 1/2 cup almond milk
- Ice cubes (optional)

Instructions:
- Combine blackberries, sliced peach, Greek yogurt, honey, and almond milk in a blender.
- Blend until smooth and creamy.
- Add ice cubes if desired and blend again for a refreshing chill.
- Pour into a glass and enjoy your Blackberry-Peach Pleasure smoothie!

Cacao Nectarine Nourishment

Ingredients:
- 1 ripe nectarine
- 1 tablespoon cacao powder
- 1 cup almond milk
- 1 tablespoon honey or maple syrup
- 1/2 banana
- Ice cubes (optional)

Instructions:
- Pit and dice the nectarine.
- In a blender, combine nectarine, cacao powder, almond milk, honey or maple syrup, and banana.
- Blend until smooth and creamy.
- Add ice cubes if desired and blend again.
- Pour into a glass and enjoy your Cacao Nectarine Nourishment!

Hazelnut-Blueberry Symphony

Ingredients:
- 1 cup blueberries (fresh or frozen)
- 1/2 cup hazelnuts
- 1 banana
- 1 cup Greek yogurt
- 1 tablespoon honey
- 1 cup almond milk

Instructions:
- Combine blueberries, hazelnuts, banana, Greek yogurt, and honey in a blender.
- Pour in almond milk to the mixture.
- Blend until smooth and creamy.
- Pour the Hazelnut-Blueberry Symphony into a glass.
- Garnish with a few whole blueberries or crushed hazelnuts if desired.
- Enjoy this delightful and nutritious smoothie!

Papaya-Mango Sunshine Splash

Ingredients
- 1 cup papaya chunks
- 1 cup mango chunks
- 1/2 cup orange juice
- 1/2 cup Greek yogurt

- 1 tablespoon honey
- Ice cubes (optional)

Instructions:
- Place papaya, mango, orange juice, Greek yogurt, and honey in a blender.
- Blend until smooth and creamy.
- Add ice cubes if desired and blend again.
- Pour into a glass and enjoy your refreshing Papaya-Mango Sunshine Splash!

Fig-Date Fusion

Ingredients:
- 1 cup fresh figs, sliced
- 1/2 cup pitted dates
- 1 banana, peeled
- 1 cup Greek yogurt
- 1 tablespoon chia seeds
- 1 cup almond milk
- Ice cubes (optional)

Instructions:
- In a blender, combine fresh figs, pitted dates, banana, Greek yogurt, and chia seeds.
- Add almond milk to the mixture.
- Blend until smooth and creamy.
- If desired, add ice cubes for a refreshing chill.

- Pour into a glass and savor the delightful Fig-Date Fusion smoothie. Enjoy!

Lemon-Raspberry Bliss

Ingredients:
- 1 cup fresh raspberries
- 1 ripe banana
- 1/2 cup Greek yogurt
- 1 tablespoon honey
- 1/2 lemon, juiced
- 1/2 cup almond milk
- Ice cubes (optional)

Instructions:
- Combine raspberries, banana, Greek yogurt, honey, and lemon juice in a blender.
- Add almond milk to the mixture.
- Blend until smooth and creamy.
- For a chilled texture, add ice cubes and blend again.
- Pour into a glass and enjoy your refreshing Lemon-Raspberry Bliss smoothie!

Cinnamon-Apple Orchard Elixir

Ingredients:
- 1 cup apple slices

- 1 banana
- 1/2 cup Greek yogurt
- 1 tablespoon honey
- 1/2 teaspoon cinnamon
- 1 cup almond milk
- Ice cubes (optional)

Instructions:
- Blend apple slices, banana, Greek yogurt, honey, and cinnamon until smooth.
- Add almond milk gradually, blending until desired consistency is reached.
- If desired, add ice cubes and blend for a refreshing chill.
- Pour into a glass, sprinkle a pinch of cinnamon on top, and enjoy the Cinnamon-Apple Orchard Elixir!

Coconut-Cherry Carnival

Ingredients:
- 1 cup frozen cherries
- 1/2 cup coconut milk
- 1 ripe banana
- 1/4 cup shredded coconut
- 1 tablespoon chia seeds
1 teaspoon honey (optional)

Instructions:
- Blend frozen cherries, coconut milk, banana, shredded coconut, and chia seeds until smooth.
- If desired, add honey for sweetness and blend again.
- Pour into a glass, garnish with a sprinkle of shredded coconut, and enjoy your Coconut-Cherry Carnival!

Turmeric-Orange Citrus Burst

Ingredients:
- 1 ripe banana
- 1 cup fresh orange juice
- 1/2 teaspoon turmeric powder
- 1/2 cup Greek yogurt
- 1 tablespoon honey
- Ice cubes (optional)

Instructions:
- In a blender, combine banana, fresh orange juice, turmeric powder, Greek yogurt, and honey.
- Blend until smooth and creamy.
- If desired, add ice cubes and blend again for a refreshing chill.
- Pour into a glass and enjoy your Turmeric-Orange Citrus Burst!

Maple-Pecan Perfection

Ingredients:
- 1 ripe banana
- 1/2 cup pecans
- 1 tablespoon maple syrup
- 1 cup Greek yogurt
- 1/2 cup almond milk
- Ice cubes (optional)

Instructions:
- Peel and slice the banana.
- In a blender, combine banana slices, pecans, maple syrup, Greek yogurt, and almond milk.
- Blend until smooth and creamy.
- Add ice cubes if desired and blend again.
- Pour into a glass and savor the Maple-Pecan Perfection!

Pineapple-Mint Mojito

Ingredients:
- 1 cup pineapple chunks
- 1 handful fresh mint leaves
- 1 lime, juiced
- 1 tablespoon honey
- 1 cup ice cubes
- 1/2 cup coconut water

Instructions:
- Blend pineapple chunks, mint leaves, lime juice, and honey until smooth.
- Add ice cubes and coconut water, then blend again until well combined.
- Pour into a glass, garnish with mint leaves or pineapple wedge, and enjoy your refreshing Pineapple-Mint Mojito!

Mango-Passion Fruit Paradise

Ingredients
- 1 cup frozen mango chunks
- 1/2 cup passion fruit juice
- 1/2 cup Greek yogurt
- 1 tablespoon honey
- 1/2 cup ice cubes

Instructions:
- Combine frozen mango chunks, passion fruit juice, Greek yogurt, and honey in a blender.
- Blend until smooth and creamy.
- Add ice cubes and blend again until the mixture is well chilled.
- Pour into a glass and enjoy your refreshing Mango-Passion Fruit Paradise smoothie!

Cranberry-Orange Almond Bliss

Ingredients:

- 1 cup cranberries (fresh or frozen)
- 1 orange, peeled and segmented
- 1 banana
- 1/4 cup almonds
- 1 cup Greek yogurt
- 1 tablespoon honey
- 1 cup ice cubes

Instructions:
- Combine cranberries, orange segments, banana, almonds, Greek yogurt, and honey in a blender.
- Blend until smooth and creamy.
- Add ice cubes and blend again until well-incorporated.
- Pour into a glass and enjoy your Cranberry-Orange Almond Bliss smoothie!

Blueberry-Coconut Cream Dream

Ingredients:
- 1 cup blueberries (fresh or frozen)
- 1/2 cup coconut cream
- 1 ripe banana
- 1 tablespoon chia seeds
- 1 teaspoon honey or maple syrup
- 1 cup almond milk
- Ice cubes (optional)

Instructions:
- Blend blueberries, coconut cream, banana, chia seeds, and sweetener until smooth.
- Gradually add almond milk while blending to achieve desired consistency.
- If desired, add ice cubes and blend until the smoothie is chilled.
- Pour into a glass, garnish with additional blueberries or coconut flakes if desired.
- Enjoy your refreshing Blueberry-Coconut Cream Dream!

Pomegranate-Raspberry Radiance

Ingredients:
- 1 cup pomegranate seeds
- 1/2 cup raspberries
- 1 banana
- 1/2 cup Greek yogurt
- 1 tablespoon honey
- 1 cup almond milk
- Ice cubes (optional)

Instructions:
- Combine pomegranate seeds, raspberries, banana, Greek yogurt, and honey in a blender.
- Add almond milk to the mixture.
- Blend until smooth and creamy.

- Optional: Add ice cubes for a refreshing chill.
- Pour into a glass and enjoy your Pomegranate-Raspberry Radiance smoothie!

Vanilla-Date Elegance

Ingredients:
- 1 ripe banana
- 1 cup almond milk
- 1/2 cup Greek yogurt
- 2 dates, pitted
- 1 teaspoon vanilla extract
- 1 tablespoon chia seeds
- Ice cubes (optional)

Instructions:
- In a blender, combine banana, almond milk, Greek yogurt, dates, and vanilla extract.
- Blend until smooth and creamy.
- Add chia seeds and blend briefly to incorporate.
- If desired, add ice cubes for a refreshing chill.
- Pour into a glass, and enjoy this elegant and nutritious Vanilla-Date Elegance Smoothie!

Strawberry-Beet Boost

Ingredients:
- 1 cup strawberries (fresh or frozen)
- 1 small beet, peeled and diced
- 1 banana

- 1/2 cup Greek yogurt
- 1 tablespoon chia seeds
- 1 cup almond milk
- Ice cubes (optional)

Instructions:
- Combine strawberries, diced beet, banana, Greek yogurt, and chia seeds in a blender.
- Add almond milk and blend until smooth.
- If desired, include ice cubes for a colder consistency.
- Pour into a glass and enjoy your Strawberry-Beet Boost – a nutritious and refreshing smoothie.

Kiwi-Mint Mojito

Ingredients:
- 2 ripe kiwis, peeled and sliced
- 1/4 cup fresh mint leaves
- 1 lime, juiced
- 1 tablespoon honey
- 1 cup ice cubes
- 1/2 cup coconut water
- 1/2 cup sparkling water

Instructions:
- In a blender, combine kiwis, mint leaves, lime juice, honey, and ice cubes.

- Add coconut water for a tropical twist.
- Blend until smooth and creamy.
- Pour the mixture into glasses.
- Top each glass with sparkling water for a refreshing fizz.
- Garnish with a kiwi slice and mint sprig.
- Stir gently and enjoy your Kiwi-Mint Mojito!

Pear-Cashew Cream Delight

Ingredients:
- 2 ripe pears
- 1/2 cup cashews (soaked)
- 1 banana
- 1 tablespoon honey
- 1 cup almond milk
- Ice cubes (optional)

Instructions:
- Peel and core the pears, then blend them with soaked cashews, banana, honey, and almond milk until smooth.
- Add ice cubes if desired and blend again for a refreshing chill.
- Pour into a glass, garnish with a slice of pear, and enjoy your Pear-Cashew Cream Delight!

Fig-Coconut Kaleidoscope

Ingredients:

- 1 cup fresh figs, stemmed and halved
- 1/2 cup shredded coconut
- 2 cups kale leaves, stems removed
- 1 banana, peeled
- 1 cup coconut water
- Ice cubes (optional)

Instructions:

- Combine figs, shredded coconut, kale, banana, and coconut water in a blender.
- Blend until smooth and creamy.
- Add ice cubes if desired and blend again.
- Pour into a glass and enjoy the vibrant Fig-Coconut Kaleidoscope smoothie!

Hazelnut-Blackberry Burst

Ingredients:

- 1 cup blackberries
- 1/2 cup hazelnuts
- 1 banana
- 1 cup Greek yogurt
- 1 tablespoon honey
- 1 cup almond milk

Instructions:

- Combine blackberries, hazelnuts, banana, Greek yogurt, and honey in a blender.
- Add almond milk to the mixture.
- Blend until smooth and creamy.
- Pour into a glass and enjoy your Hazelnut-Blackberry Burst!

Papaya-Ginger Zinger

Ingredients

- 1 cup ripe papaya chunks
- 1/2 inch fresh ginger, peeled and chopped
- 1 banana
- 1/2 cup plain Greek yogurt
- 1 tablespoon honey
- 1 cup ice cubes
- 1/2 cup coconut water

Instructions:

- Combine papaya chunks, chopped ginger, banana, Greek yogurt, honey, and ice cubes in a blender.
- Add coconut water for a refreshing twist.
- Blend until smooth and creamy.
- Pour into a glass and enjoy your invigorating Papaya-Ginger Zinger Smoothie!

Orange-Carrot Citrus Symphony

Ingredients:
- 2 oranges, peeled and segmented
- 1 large carrot, peeled and chopped
- 1 cup Greek yogurt
- 1 tablespoon honey
- 1 cup ice cubes

Instructions:
- Combine oranges, chopped carrot, Greek yogurt, and honey in a blender.
- Blend until smooth and creamy.
- Add ice cubes and blend again until the mixture is chilled and smooth.
- Pour into a glass and enjoy the refreshing Orange-Carrot Citrus Symphony!

Cinnamon-Plum Perfection

Ingredients:
- 2 ripe plums, pitted and sliced
- 1 banana, peeled
- 1 cup Greek yogurt
- 1/2 teaspoon ground cinnamon
- 1 tablespoon honey
- 1/2 cup almond milk
- Ice cubes (optional)

Instructions:

- In a blender, combine sliced plums, banana, Greek yogurt, ground cinnamon, honey, and almond milk.
- Blend until smooth and creamy.
- If desired, add ice cubes and blend again for a refreshing chill.
- Pour into a glass and garnish with a sprinkle of cinnamon.
- Enjoy your Cinnamon-Plum Perfection!

Peach-Basil Breeze

Ingredients:

- 1 cup frozen peaches
- 1 banana
- 1/2 cup Greek yogurt
- 1/2 cup orange juice
- 1 tablespoon honey
- Fresh basil leaves (to taste)

Instructions:

- Combine frozen peaches, banana, Greek yogurt, orange juice, and honey in a blender.
- Blend until smooth and creamy.
- Add fresh basil leaves to the mixture and blend briefly for a burst of herbal freshness.

- Pour into a glass and enjoy your Peach-Basil Breeze!

Minty Pineapple Spinach Surprise

Ingredients:
- 1 cup fresh pineapple chunks
- 1 cup baby spinach leaves
- 1/2 cup mint leaves
- 1 banana, peeled
- 1/2 cup Greek yogurt
- 1 tablespoon honey
- 1 cup ice cubes
- 1/2 cup water

Instructions:
- Combine pineapple chunks, spinach leaves, mint leaves, banana, Greek yogurt, and honey in a blender.
- Add ice cubes for a refreshing chill.
- Pour in water for the desired consistency.
- Blend until smooth and creamy.
- Pour into a glass and enjoy your Minty Pineapple Spinach Surprise!